WOOF! WOOF!

ROB A. MACKENZIE
Woof! Woof! Woof!

SALT

CROMER

PUBLISHED BY SALT PUBLISHING 2023

2 4 6 8 10 9 7 5 3 1

First published in Great Britain in 2023 by
Salt Publishing Ltd
12 NORWICH ROAD, CROMER, NORFOLK NR27 0AX UNITED KINGDOM

www.saltpublishing.com

Salt Publishing Limited Reg. No. 5293401

A CIP catalogue record for this book is available from the British Library

ISBN 978 1 78463 280 9 (Paperback edition)

Typeset in Sabon by Salt Publishing

Printed and bound in Great Britain by Clays Ltd, Elcograf S.p.A

to Medha Singh
a true friend

Contents

Woof! Woof! Woof!

The Dog

. . . and the dog barked when no one was listening.

It barked outside the Tesco Local day and night.
Its leash had long bedecked the crumbling bollard.

> According to the *Daily Mail*, they mixed meths
> and cheap red wine, topped it with Brasso
> strained through a nylon stocking for extra zing.

> Only then could they hear the dog bark
> and understand its warning.

The dog barked at every slide of the sliding doors.

Beats seeped briefly from the tannoy
to shadows outside, to nodding heads.

> They drank and their throats were burning
> like the burning throat of the barking dog
> as if prophets from the same scripture.

But the dog had no books in its barking.

The dog barked and its bereavement settled
like a winding-sheet on each burdened trolley.

> They were flushed, angry and knew their curses
> irked passers-by, who heard in them
> the barks of a burning dog.

In silence, a woman forgot her PIN,
a man waited glumly for approval.

The dog died and the bollard looked strange.
The shoppers were shocked by how much
they missed what they'd never heard.

The Book

'And we tore dark squares, thick pages
From the Book of Fire'
– GEORGE MACKAY BROWN, 'Peat Cutting'

The book dug into the dark beginning as a burning dog
    might chase its comet tail, white hot and haphazard
        in a cloud of steam, or a crowd kettled by the force

of blunt instruments, wag wag wag: the sway of it,
    the stagger, the collapse, the page turned in one
        mass semi-circular slump – thump! crash! – bodies

bellowing flame, but only yesterday the 26 bus
    looked like a beast surplus to the apocalypse,
        its windows smashed and tyres torn into spaghetti;

the book clothed itself with that bus and then
    undressed again, the world continued as it had
        ever been, the new normal cut in shattering glass,

the big bang, the free-wheeling ride everyone
    says they want and then spends a lifetime trying
        to avoid, the book of inner life that's so fascinating

to no one whomsoever, certainly not to vandals
    throwing boulders at buses and ripping their knives
        into wheels to the honking laughter of land rovers,

honk! honk! honk! perhaps that was the vandals . . .
    they're all just one happy family in the book going
        up in smoke, the vandals and land rovers shooting

the shit together, whatever that means, it's like
    with like or perhaps like like with like, the level
        of simile, not reality, in the shush! the swish!

the pages turning, the pages of the book – shush!
    swish! – emporium of ideas that will never be any
        use to anyone, and whatever my story, the book

will tell it differently; it will catch up with the past
    before I know it, wordlessly – woof! woof! woof! –
        barking prophecies, entirely of events that have

already happened, as nothing hasn't happened
    already, and there is so much to discover in what
        we think we already have read within the bonfire

of information the book contained, which now
    feels uncontainable, spreading in disintegration
        like a dog's shadow escaping the confines of its dog,

dragged from its proper place by the kerbside
    or basket, silhouette sniffer now with palpable
        ambition to be an upwardly mobile status symbol

of freedom – badges! labels! photo shoots! –
    worn lightly until lightly worn and then easily
        discarded like a slogan that has served its purpose

of buying in, like the inspirational Mandela
    fabricated quotation brought to you by Google
        with land rover pop-up and magic tree carrying

precise scents from Donald Trump's upper neck
    swiftly reclassified as illegal chemical weapon:
        stock for novichok, radioactive soup for the soul-

less spirit; the book extends its sympathies,
    withdraws its condolence, proclaims neutrality
        and its impossibility, sits on the fence and falls

randomly on one side or the other, but always
    falls, takes the fence down with it, and leaves
        the hostile fighters drawing fresh dividing lines

to fight over: the broken shell of the 26 bus
    a meaningless boundary where they pitch
        boulders into territorial cairns, or like the dog

cocking its leg promiscuously at a scattering
    of lampposts; a similar excitement at being
        named in the book's microscopic footnotes,

less appendix than appendicitis, flared up
    and hosed down, emerging like a writer whose
        emerging is continual and perennially moot,

a mosquito buzzing distinctively from ear
    to ear, chapter to chapter, isolated even
        from subplots and tangents destined to be

dumped at first proofs, the book primed
    to re-establish the forgotten in ecstatic
        pulp briquettes, combustible biomass,

flames rising high but with lower grade
    warmth than the endlessly recyclable
        wooden traditions the book so loves

to run with, and then cut – thick pages
    globbed together, hellish papier mâché
        gloopy oblongs, like plinths prepared

for abandoned statues, oyez! oyez! oyez!
    The town criers roar, *Is Language Dead?*
        in what might as well be an unknown

pre-Etruscan tongue rumbling from buses,
    as rocks are flung, the book scribbles on,
        and every era proclaims a golden age.

What I'd Prefer

'The Book of Revelation? Nah. I prefer the Revelation of Books'
—ROSS MCCLEARY, Twitter

Ross has preferences. It is important to respect a preference, even
    when it is wrong,
although Ross is not wrong, not entirely or even a little, because
    the Book of Revelation
is a book and therefore subject to revelation and both statements
    are true without

recourse to Nah, which could just as well be Yeah or even Yeah!!!
    Or any other word:
Submarine, Bitumen, Steak. I prefer the Revelation of Books.
    Although often what feels
like revelation is only what we already think rattled back to us in
    unfamiliar forms;

why bitumen would be an especially interesting mode of epiphany
    due to its lack
of promise, because everything it has to reveal is surface and, like
    Hugh Grant in
About a Boy, has no obvious depths, except when that is proved
    wrong, as it was

in Hugh's case, one of the film's most important revelations: people
    resist revealing
themselves to themselves. What I'd prefer is a book of Hugh, open
    and leafed through,
to the hue of revelation as a distant sun. I don't know if Ross
    would agree, but I think

it's possible for people to disagree and not overheat. Of course, I
    realise *not* everyone
agrees with that: some people throw tantrums if others follow or
    like tweets written by
those they disagreed with about something completely different
    months or years ago

and insist on compliance to their demands. They are like charred
    cabins hosting local
apocalypses, rare steaks on a hot grill sweating blood – all for
    opinions, the importance
of which remain unclear. What I'd prefer is submarines descending
    to the murk and just

staying there, all Ringo yellow, the only way it's possible to see the
    world as it truly is
through our eyes. I'm fine if Ross opts for hue over Hugh even if
    losing the argument
slices my heart open. It means so much to me, I now realise. Nah,
    not really! I will note

in this poem the names of anyone who won't reveal themselves in
    the stand-up mirror
where I capture *me* – a book, I mean, as I'm told we all have one in
    us awaiting a final
chapter – mainly unreadable, unwriteable, and not a story we'd ever
    choose to tell.

Stationary Wagon

words yoked together
like parties to a bad
fifties' marriage,
a symbol going
nowhere except
out of time
and, as symbols
depend on context
for meaning, also
blurry and suspicious –
the wagon unable to
fulfil its only function
by the old-fashioned
headmaster adjective
governing by power
and disproportionate
anxiety of influence;
even then, mainly
in abstract as words
on paper, or two
railway carriages,
neither possessing
an engine – a perfect
advantage only for
the former – and here
the literary critics
find coded jealousy
and anger against
mobile phones
and other shifting

technological apparatus
providing illusions of
movement, progress –
they still can't decide
whether the simulated
gallop and trot
a rocking horse,
nuanced yet compromised,
delivers on the spot
is exactly the same
or polar opposite
to how definition
turns, unturns, in
a stationary wagon.

The Loop

'Nothing is funnier than unhappiness, I grant you that ...'
SAMUEL BECKETT, *Endgame*

All songs come to an end, except
the very worst, which *insist*,
stuck in a loop, messing up your brain
with a heart of processed cheese.

The very worst verse insists:
'Agadoo', 'Achy Breaky Heart',
a heart of processed cheese:
'Barbie Girl', 'I'm Too Sexy',

'Agadoo', 'Achy Breaky Heart' . . .
the riffs repeat, you're trapped:
'Barbie Girl', 'I'm Too Sexy' –
just as you find a distraction

the riffs repeat, you're trapped
inside their heap, up to your neck.
Just as you find a distraction,
you begin to laugh – at suffering

inside *their* heap, up to your neck
in 'Macarena' and 'Ob la di ob la da'.
You begin to laugh at suffering
the world had stopped laughing at.

'O, Macarena' and 'Ob la di ob la da',
novel for a time, but novel no more.
The world had stopped laughing at
tragedy on repeat, tragedy on repeat,

novel for a time, but novel no more.
The Bee Gees pipe all-night soprano:
'Tragedy' on repeat, 'Tragedy' on repeat.
Let's face it, it's all you've ever heard.

The Bee Gees pipe all-night soprano,
but all songs come to an end except,
let's face it, everything you've heard,
stuck in a loop, messing up your brain.

The British

The mood, as the nation caught fire,
lifted at the sight of a football bouncing
towards a curiously undefined goal.

It brought cheer to think of themselves
as victors, without having to think
of who the victims were or whether

victory was worth the heat awaiting them,
while pundits did doctorates on national
pride, a natural prelude to humiliation:

the invention of Oatibix an all-time
cereal low, the new line in High Street
riot gear now as 'British' as Earl Grey

tea on the lawn, watching the chump
at silly point knock himself out with
the thrill of imminent concussion:

doggedly British as refusing to believe
kangaroos exist, because ten blokes
without passports haven't seen one;

slapstick British as the feminist chap
struggling to set up an ironing board
but writing tweets on male toxicity;

shapeshift British as the supermarket
rebrand of *doughnut* peaches as *flat*
to avoid glamorising bakery treats;

impartially British as the arsonists
insisting they'd turned *England* to ash
when they reached the tip of Unst.

There was nothing left to burn but
swells north of Britain, where waves
disrespected rights of encroachment,

slapping each other like frightened
schoolkids, unwilling to recognise
the fluid borders of flickering lives.

Reporting Scotland

Laura Miller is reading the news:
gloomy footage of handymen with the stomach
for human offal, boil-in-the-bag or barbecued black;
an inside story on the left winger
warming the bench for Bonnyrigg Rose, who dreamed
of glory with Cowdenbeath, and fell to earth;
exclusive chat with the typecast hardman D-lister,
flick-knife in one hand, stookie emblazoned with Glaswegian
insults guiding the other to acts of rehearsed abandon;
another pyrophoric day of nationwide drama:
Tory and Labour councillors dancing like drunks
to celebrate their precious union
in eternal opposition, stopping only to watch
Laura Miller reading the news
and this time my life is served up for civic debate
like a deep-fried haggis buffet for a company
of vegan dieticians, all of them swallowing
and retching, swallowing and retching, swallowing
my facts, fakes, flukes and flops
until the best boys, boom operators, vision mixers and dolly grips
have left the building and the studio lies
derelict apart from the incongruous ceiling fan's *thunk thunk*
and Laura Miller reading the news
to that one fan, in perfect rhythm, a left right
quick march *thunk thunk* story about a band
of chimpanzees who typed a single line
of the 'old hundredth' backwards, after three thousand years of
    glorious
failure – *Scottish* chimpanzees, the perfect, happy penultimate
before the headline recap: positive notes

to inspire a song, perhaps even a national anthem
cordially agreed on, if only for seconds of heel-kicking
bliss on Bannockburn; then, departure with the weather
forecast of comedy and horror, its attuned
choir of onlookers left to mull the moment, to lull
the blues, to serenade each simmering tomorrow
when Laura Miller is reading the news.

Slates of the Nation

LYRICAL

There are worse places to look for guidance
than Mark E. Smith's lyrics. Do you need work?
Become a container driver, a Sparta F.C.
ballboy, a maker of huckleberry masks:

I've already written a poetry book
with a jawbone of Fall allusions. I don't want
to make more formerly enthusiastic
readers think I'm now an acroamatic cunt

so, here's advice from the primary offices:
government flunkies recommend the supine
should access compulsory paralysis
and hard-working Scousers read *The Sun*.

Bite, click, fruit farms need picked. You must apply.
This article will obscure precisely why.

THE CRITIC SPEAKS
for Francesca Peacock and *Joelle Taylor*

This article explains precisely why
I loathe contemporary verse. Not all of it,
just poems beneath my notice, the empty
shelves for books the prizewinner would write
if she were someone else: Selima Hill
or Wendy Cope, dead ringers in my head,
give or take a chasm of darkness. I will
argue my case till they're blue in the face. Or dead,

and that has made all the difference. Somehow
when I think of poets dead, even those yet
alive and (forsooth!) unread, a tragedy
of Shakespearian import weighs upon my brow.
I resolve to read J's book tonight! Instead,
I snore through *Henry IV, Part 1*, on TV.

YESTERDAY
for the brilliant M. C.

I soiréed through *Henry IV, Part 1*, on TV.
Prince Harry acted the hard man, Falstaff
the whiner, Percy couldn't master his fury.
Politics as usual. My advice: never laugh
at power, nil by mealymouth, don't count your likes.
When the crunch comes, the likes disappear.
Most poets revert to haunting open mics
and spend hours refashioning their hair.

Matthew Caley approached me in my dreams
and told me all the birds were going to eat
themselves. He told me prophecy is easy
if trumpeted from the past. The past now seems
like a prefab future, where I write and rewrite
songs already written by Lennon & McCartney.

DON'T SING

Songs already written by Lennon & McCartney
sound original when my brain's choir
tinkles the oasis and wails them off-key
like an incandescent canary. I'm on fire
these days. I've hatched enough for a sophomore
White Album I'll call the *Eggshell-White Album* –
'Back in the U.S.A.', 'Born in the U.S.S.R.' –
two singles to rival Gallagher and Albarn
but it's just my imagination running away
without me. I'm a hound-dog crying at
a winking satellite; high time I'm poisoned
or stoned in a pseudo-biblical conspiracy,
unearthed decades later, like a thought
that strayed; missing, presumed abandoned.

LOST LEAD

Missing, presumed abandoned,
amid reed, nettlebed or quicksand –
attached or unattached to dog
is unclear in the aromatic smog.

A wild-goose chase for a lead suspends
the solitary *woof* always downwind
of sniffers' and snoopers' deathless hunt
for buckle and strap – unbuckled, absent.

If, some day, they track down not
the signified but the sign of it
set free from human discipline,
they'll drop the evidence. If a stone

rouses a tomb or avalanche
they'll see nothing, call it a hunch.

Nothing. I know nothing. Call it a hunch
but often I'd rather spot the nothing that
presents itself like a gift-wrapped curse
than get caught in the act of seeing straight.

I pace the streets, my head bowed in prayer
before rockpools of dogshit, gum and vomit;
epiphany lurks in the sentimental everywhere;
you find waste and surplus, I see god-deposit.

Your pain is great material for my worst verse –
the metre goes berserk, I'm too stressed to care.
'Is it terminal or interminable?' I ask over lunch
and rewrite the world in degrees of laissez-faire.

The birds eat themselves, while I contemplate
my need for veneration as a poet.

PLACE YOUR BETS

A need for veneration? As a poet,
I've weathered the dark night of the overspill
for decades, a hard shoulder where the lost
leads lie, their dogs kennelled among parallel
constellations of winking amber lights,
while novelists wolf down the motorway
to fame and fingerfood. Listen, I'll waste
my life in alliteration, in metonymy,
if it kills me. It beats working full-tilt
as creative writing tutor, librarian
or whisky priest; beats going down the pits
and once there never coming up again;
beats trading souls for politics and crime –
my flutter through the dim arcs of fame.

THE GOLDEN CALF

One flutter through the slim arcs of fame,
the fifteen minutes reduced to two or three –
no one can match Warhol's attention span.
Do you have the X Factor? That quality
of indefinable élan that dresses up
accretional vanity as popular demand?
Everyone does! The gospel of Campbell's soup
endlessly reproduced. Seek and ye shall find
last week in this week's canned applause,
the fire of empires lit and doused, headlines
forged by ancient Latin scribes whose gods
still extract blood from sacrificial wines.
Products flush by. The factory has closed.
The latest tribute merchandise explodes.

BLAST

The latest tribute merchandise explodes:
no laud, no honour, no late tribulation.
Yesterday and today spat platitudes –
how to package the spirit of a nation –
the I'm Alright Jacks so psyched to leave
their oversized baggage for tomorrow's blast
of shrapnel and glitter. Time is less a thief,
more a killer. There's no time left to rust.

A dog whistle's just a whistle without
a dog. The fascist wags a fashionable ass
and buttery cyst. God is a poet with gout.
A storybook draws a blank without a story.
A bossanova will never move a boss.
A factory's just a fact without a Tory.

DANCE DANCE DANCE

A factory is fucked whenever a Tory
mimes a bossanova with the poodles
to illustrate the economy. Don't worry,
there will be rationalization, oodles
of it, and plenty of cockamamie wack –
when a factory dies, the home secretary
dons a hard hat, appropriates a broomstick
for the photo op, employs CGI trickery
for each staged sympathy crash-landing.
The bossanova gathers pace, then slumps;
the poodles carry on solo, demanding
compulsory muzzles, tax relief on dumps
fired at the gutter, a purge on canine rights.
The last creature standing puts out the lights.

Pack up Your Troubles

When the last lamplighter puts out the lights
and Mary Poppins pops her clogs in rhythm,
it's no surprise they take the magic with them.
I'm left with spells cast in stone, love bites
without the bite, rainbows in monochrome.
I tell myself it couldn't last. It's not shit
to dream big, to be on this pointless list
with many grafters I admire, humdrum

but hopeful, waving a toy Harry Potter
wand at billionaires with fingers on
their triggers, and only a little futile.
I find a metal guru, eat myself fitter,
light a candle to scare off Armageddon.
A workman orders me to smile, smile, smile.

THE BLAME

A workman orders me to smile, smile, smile;
'It might never happen!' His optimism
is heart-rending, undeterred by sarcasm.
I want to kiss him on the mouth, beguile
him with sad tales of emotional torpor
overcome by this impulsive instant.
If I were a woman, that's what he'd want –
a fantasy of power, a smiling whore.

He explains the germane term is 'sex worker'.
If I watched more subtitled films, I'd learn
how words and women translate. I blame my narrator,
who blames the standoffish author neither
of us admire, a fly-by-night pseudonym.
We're sniffing out his misleading persona.

SEARCH PARTY

We're sniffing out a misleading persona,
the dog and I, his nose pressed to each cold
trail like a tracking cookie: bespectacled
boxer, crafty glasnost, Calvinist porno,
lost minotaur, a tail he chases that twists
endlessly labyrinthine; an internet
of otherness. Scroll, click or urinate,
the wall extends, the feed is a multiplex

for internecine conflict, cinematic –
sure! – but lacking direction, too reliant
on popcorn and crackly packet flimflam.
The dog gnaws at stains or chews a brick;
I've ripped up the only flowering houseplant.
It's killing us, this sweet compulsive boredom.

I Never Play Basketball Now

It's killing us, this sweet compulsive boredom,
watching the game: dog from the laundry basket,
me from the sofa. Sport is the ultimate
reality TV. We leave the team
to win (or lose) for us. We contemplate
(or vegetate) on what we might have been
had we measured more than five foot seven
and lived the dream we sleep through or spectate.

It's all about the fans. It's us who pay
to subsidise star power, or banish it
to orbits remote from back page headlines:
archery, polo, ferret legging, shinty,
the posthumous endurance of Mark E. Smith –
there are worse places to look for guidance.

CORONATION

These poems have explained precisely why
songs were written by Lennon & McCartney;
why factories are fucked whenever a Tory
soirées through *Henry IV, Part 1*, on TV.

They've sniffed out each misleading persona.
There are worse places to look for guidance
that strayed; missing, presumed abandoned.
I *know* nothing. Nothing! Call it a hunch.

I flutter through the dim arcs of fame
and seek true veneration as a poet.
My latest tribute sonnet crown explodes.
It kills with a sweet compulsive boredom.

A workman orders me to smite, smite, smite
The last editor standing puts out the light.

Meteor

The size of what we had to say
was a meteor plunging through

a universe's outer edge,
as far from sunlight and gravitational pull

as Pluto the planet is from Pluto the dog,
the surface of Hades from the surface of Disney,

a thin slash in the preacher's thick robe
high in the pulpit, swaying

yet unswaying, a sashay down the biblical
catwalk in a land where dogwalk

is currency – the bins thick with poopbag,
the channels frothing with greyhound humour,

pitbull tone, boxer clench and sidestep and swing,
brimful with peptalk as a halftime tunnel

at seven nil down, the crowd one man
and his pup, waiting to mow

a pitch medalled with shattered glass –
hopeless, you might think, a non-league art,

a gallery of images for light
years unvisited, until the lonely tourist

rock senses atmosphere, catches fire and scores
a direct hit, the building from a godlike

perspective opening up, like a flower
or flare, a giant, silent crater

that, aeons from now, scientists
visit with questions we can't even imagine.

Adventures

'We have heard of such towns – Aberdeen, Grimsby, London'
GEORGE MACKAY BROWN, 'Vikings: Two Harp Songs'

These days, I have adventures with smoked paprika
by kitchen striplight, marinating chicken with garlic,
olive oil, cumin, coriander, black pepper, turmeric.

I hear that one can buy the ingredients in Grimsby,
that central London has already piloted electricity
and microwave ready meals. There, it's still very

possible to plug in, switch on, and experience
total lack of power, but I demand my thruppence
worth. Here, at Leith's cutting edge, the blue rinse

is back in fashion, safety pins are driven through
eyeballs, and I have branded a designer stew.
The musos have given up pontificating on new

music, as a revolutionary gesture. They say it
died as art in a club in Aberdeen, 1968.
They're now into fluffing the perfect omelette.

'Omelette! *See it, say it, sorted*!' is their slogan.
Eggs intimidate me, their hard faces. I login
to egg sites and their bias against chicken

is a turn-off. I wish smoked paprika restored
my high. Where is London anyway? I scoured
a map, found only Luton. No, I'm not bored.

Exchange/Gift

a grain of truth for a pocket of opinion

spray of flowers for a spattered window

a gram of weight for a ten tonne influence

single anchovy for heaving trawler

a slice of life for a cooling loaf

suspicion of riches for romance of poverty

a pint topped up for a gallon of bitterness

helium of laughter for uranium of zeal

an open door for a hiss of cynics

ideas above your station for modesty of dreams

a thimble of imagination for an oilfield roar

Norwegian noise trials for popular demand

a millimetre made for a mile back consumed

conspicuous eccentricity for established applause

The Tangents

Rejoice in the tangents,
their tangerine tang.

In unseasonal orange,
through the veiny
urban grid,
the God of Blood
predestines cars to crash
like hi-vis jackets
skidding into
low res twilight.

In bar after bar
fiery neon signs
go suddenly cold.

Stick to the wide
deodorized avenues
and you'll find
mainly plane trees
and silver Fiestas
slowing to twenty.

But ride the alleys
and shady lanes,
perfectly aligned
Irn Bru bottles
lie splintered from
drive-by buckshot.

Rejoice in the choice,
in the chivvying chase.

A traffic light, stuck
on amber:
a modern city's
wireless, handless
clock.

There's no time
by the time
the bus wheels into
the terminus
for raising fingers at
traffic cones
intent on diversion.

The bluest insults
usually coalesce
imaginatively, hours
after incitement.

Rejoice in the quarrelling,
the calming quality of cooks.

A battered golden
Mars Bar treat
for all the family
rolling home from
Rail Dust county.

They career off
the maps and back
on again, hugging
the sand tracks
tight as ticks.

Irregular thumping
of dicky hearts,
their hymn to life.

Shelter

I've spent aeons in this shelter, waiting for
the only working lamp-post in the street
to leave the darkness

unpunctuated, and a life sentence served
finally, either like the bus that came early
or rusted in the station –

inconsequential as academic revolutionaries
clustered in a Costa, all of them thinking
themselves Sartres, puffing

out their chests like badly-designed blowfish,
chewing *pain au raisin* because it's French
and fresh and they can

imagine they're cast in a classic by Truffaut
or Eric Cantona – a reverie interrupted by
rain beating Calvinist

psalms on the shelter roof because this is
not Paris but Prestonpans and the last bus
careened past what

seems like years ago and left me spinning
in slipstream, dragging my ragdoll feet
around the stop

like a drunk Morris dancer: scattered cans
and bottles testify to my indefensible
undoing, my lack

of strategy, which was, of course, a strategy,
not distraction or unfinished business
compartmentalised

between commas, absences, work-related
drinks, months when the autobiographical
film director on film

asked me daily what it was like to date her –
every twitch in the bed logged and evaluated
by fans, followers

and 24/7 stalkers, every influence monetized:
my transubstantiating hairstyle, shoe colour
and prim heterodoxy

suddenly all the rage and therefore ripe for
public evisceration, those online snivellers
with moralistic cruelty

'holding accountable' flaws they find evident
in me, others, yet most evident but missed
or unacknowledged

in themselves, gnomes crouched in shelters
exactly like mine, forged from the twin
flames of neoshitic

perspex and artex, invisible to the literally-
minded eye and to the lost number 11
which bulleted past,

lights off, like a planet bamboozled by
its own elliptical passage, its lonely arc
a bum steer from

the mollifying jollies of the inner circle's
eternal parallel, but perfect for this space –
solid as a lemon

glacier fruit suspended in formaldehyde,
ridiculous as a single-use, half-empty
plastic water bottle –

this shelter would be a multi-million dollar
sensation if suspended from a nail or granted
a thin atmosphere,

dumb graffiti and enough bathroom facilities
to raise it to the level of an averagely neglected
town centre: Airdrie,

Pompeii, anywhere south of Leicestershire,
instead of this imaginative site where I wait,
my unbroken line

of one, still queuing out of habit: the last
skittle standing before a giant bowling ball
fucks up the spare,

the sweep bar freezes, and the pinsetter
malfunction is declared a permanent fault,
only in the sense

that a watching kettle never boils, a cliché
that never fulfils its potential, and leaves me
waiting in this shelter

for aeons until the working lamppost arranges
the darkness still to be discovered by those
who currently live there.

Principles

Let's say you're dead against chains –
start a petition, demand a boycott,
shout out independent alternatives
through a loudhailer, spend long
afternoons inside a sandwich board
warning against the twin evils
of capitalism and commodity
but then accept a position as
poet in residence at Wetherspoons
and justify it by writing enraged
poems about the environmental
fallout from teabags – how blind
drunk will you need to get before
you recognise yourself again?

Mouth

Unplanned architecture:
a grand 18th century
Georgian townhouse
flanked by a gothic
cathedral, art deco
upside-down tower,
a score of brutalist
concrete blocks
yellowing like pages
of second-hand books
and behind them
a demented skatepark
bowl ramp flapping
pinkly, dangerously
toward the sanitized
probe, which scrapes
evidence of decay,
ashes, dying tongues:
smouldering cavities
like braziers balanced
loosely on dystopian
landfill sites – a city
filmed in saliva
praying for a Listerine
flood, a washed-up
saviour to drill
the scorched terrain
like a kiss.

Homework

This is not a house, more a project,
homework; not a home and not work
for that matter, more a frieze cobbled
together for fun, with glue, with glitter.
It smells of damp burgundy curtains
that repel the light like underworld
Rottweilers. Sometimes I hear them
bark from their windows at passing
architects, who see there's a job here
needing done but balk at doing it.
They stick to plans on parchment,
theoretical safety: bedrooms without
floors, attics with ceilings the shape
of bicycles, aspirational extensions
with blackout blinds. The curtains
flutter – like butterflies, some said,
but more like cornered brutes
prepared to spring. I know they
will never allow walls and roofs,
doors and log fires, to move in
and beat back the cold and rain.
The builders keep telling me
it is finished, was finished long ago,
but no one has ever knocked on
anything but air or rang a bell
to interrupt my practical dreams.

After Maths

The last class over,
I was a born again
believer in formula-
free expression;
no longer choked by
the overpowering
multiplex algebra
of Mrs Inwood's
botanic stench;
or governed by
fear of blackboards,
of trig diagrams
cribbed from
flat-pack instructions,
of tangents and sines
enigmatic as
my grin alight
under interrogation,
of digits multiplying
like fruit flies whose
negativity to the power
of god the chalk,
squeak and fractional
dust-up meant that
my equations never
revealed mysteries
or offered more
than slapdash balance;
always remaining
marooned, measuring

in millipede feet
the mean distance
between two abstract
points of view,
which now feels
more negotiable –
the world outside
the classroom
and lecture hall,
I know, it is
all mathematics,
no less complex
for seeming not so:
thuggish panellists
at loggerheads
over long division,
underground
figures sponsored
by state approval,
bodies spiralling
from the jubilant
rush of last orders
to bottled spirits
in drab kitchens –
the imperceptibly
sheer slide
from peak hypotenuse –
all still feeling
invincible, articulate
as budding Hamlets

rehearsing soliloquys
for the final act's
supernumerary
aftermath.

Goldfish

I ogled a goldfish in its crystal shell.
The fish was dead, the gold was Ruskoline.
The fish circled lyrically on a movie reel,
while Coldplay honked out *Gold* on a trombone.

The film was *The Matrix* directed by a fish.
Gold hook or silver hook? Mirage or reality?
The Golden Fry crumbled like poor old Elvis
and set an elfish argument underway:

Hopkins and Hill squared up at Goldengrove –
fishes out of water, they traded slaps.
Comedy gold, like prog rock! Barely a shove,
both were out cold, like fish battered with clubs,

but banged out a golden age of rock-and-roll,
the film suggests, in a fishy twist of the tale.

Portobello Beach

The tide is in, and here's the haar
    go sad or sweet or riotous with beer
but still, they're licking ice-poles on
the shingle, stripped to their underwear
    despite the pincering frost,
ready to welcome another year of stone
by diving head first.

Easter weekend and empty vessels
    go sad or sweet or riotous with beer
line up with open gobs of sand
to swallow the insubordinate drizzle:
    breaking news, the same
illusions and conspiracies, the underhand
shifting of blame.

It must be the summer of polka dot pink
    go sad or sweet or riotous with beer
and upturned stracciatella cones;
the only solution is to drink
    until the sadness lifts
in waves, wave by wave by wave, and soon
finds itself adrift.

The fish are battered for the deep-fat fryer
    go sad or sweet or riotous with beer
the sunbathers measure the depths
they'll keep within. Autumn flares
    scarlet in the sky;
tomorrow will be too cold to take a breath
either on land or sea.

The Good News

The long weekend felt like one massive street party.
Wine bottles and pointy sandwiches spilled from
Skaw to Land's End. We toasted a promised land

of bumper crops, plus-size cucumber and aubergine.
The sandwiches were experimental; genetic editors
had conjured the skeletal vegetables from the fillet

of fleshy DNA. All good news, according to official
climate change-denying experts who spun science
to clone more climate change-denying experts

who denied the existence of expertise and cited
parliamentary white papers, and by white papers
they meant blank sheets. They ripped up the old

templates and furnished temples to refusal
with hulled antimatter. Nothing, they said, was
more than three days old and three days later

said the same again: the dinosaurs were just
God's witchy trick, fossils the commercial arm
of His pottery barn. God liked to wind us up

like prehistoric clocks. Deadlines came and went,
went and came, like one-shot resurrections
recycled in revolving doors. Nothing was in it

for the long haul. The supermarkets stocked
Nothing Day bric-a-brac to raise awareness
of nothing beyond a sponsored veneration

of empty shelves which, last we heard, overtook
Black Friday as the top apology for evolution.
If only we'd stick to mass destruction forever . . .

went the slogan, prompting stiff competition
to finish the sentence, but no entries were of
sufficient standard. It remained as incomplete

as history: those tragedies to come for which
we were unrehearsed. The tannins we drank
left notes of milk and honey on our tongues.

Arthur's Seat

A thousand candles of gorse
fizzed from volcanic roots
like a church floodlit
by vanity, or the buzz
of taxis vying for
dominance at the crossroads.

The city below took the brightness
as a taunt,
shrouded the stars
in neon. The gorse spat
flames like empty prayers
for stonechat and yellowhammer.

Shore

Here by chance
a gift a plague

we settle for
unsettling deliveries

waves longing
for stillness

promised beyond
the horizon

drag words bottles
canisters rust oil

sewage beach
a whale waves

unable to deny
progress agency

compare the ancients'
use of the passive

voice to designate
acts of God

luring the bait
of effect to cause

wished for
or plotted yes

what floats
is floated

what washes up
is washed up

empty pasta
salad trays

the every
day discounted

Waterfront

'How should I find a way back
To the waterfront of Trondheim?'
GEORGE MACKAY BROWN, 'Voyager'

I approach the final gathering at the waterfront of Trondheim,
where all who judged harshly will be judged in turn. Each step

forward is a journey through the past, although also
a final gathering. The orators expected

fire and brimstone and instead find a carnival of snowmen
and snowwomen making the journey on melting torsos

as if time were short and not a continual lessening
eternity. The old life's phobia of fire

has become an ache for what they no longer possess:
fear. It stalks the clocks like a crow-pecked scarecrow

in growing corn, not the inferno they believed in.
Human nature longs for the stability

of orators: the right-wing uniformed juntas and their heirs
the left-wing puritans holding beliefs, and apologies for them,

to the flame. Together, they salute
Trondheim's spotless fjord and orate, spontaneously,

to the snowfolk they always resembled, like convex mirrors,
ruined cathedrals, or this – my mythical vision of Trondheim –

magnified in the mind, until essentially divine,
                if gods can resemble graven images,

shifts of snow, without being projections – rather, as real
as existence preceding essence, or as populist slogans

skewering complex truths. We slide forward,
                the scales shift, and I find myself

fallen and adrift on the Old Town Bridge, which sways
under the weight of self-assured progress and delusion

of advance, racked between melting hands and
                words deleting words from history.

Map of a Cow

It should have been easy to travel from the east
gate to the west, but I have a dark northern mind
and drifted towards the early afternoon twilight.
The path lost its bearings somewhere between
the Glasshouse, the Arboretum and the Chinese
Hillside, and soon had become a field as vast
as a football pitch, eerily floodlit, with one
dappled cow munching on the centre circle.
I saw at once the cow was my way out of there.
Its left flank had a blob shaped something like
Romania, detailed intersectional bus routes
from town to town, alleyways which promised
both danger and no regrets, a region where
only Torlakian was spoken. For the first time
in my life, I made a travel plan: booked hotels,
reserved seats on empty train carriages, filled
Tupperware boxes with salad and dull lumps
of gammon. No roast beef though. I named
the cow Pat, spilled fresh water in its trough,
and left, not stopping to question what a cow
was doing in the Edinburgh Botanic Gardens,
or how I emerged after only fifteen days on
Brandon Street and ordered a cappuccino
and pain au raisin from the Blue Bear Café.

Virus

Mice mob
the footbridge
from Saughton Mains
to Carrick Knowe,
a safe
eighty metre span
between coughs.
The sky
moths over.
Toddlers play
dead on beached
trampolines.
The screen
pandemic
may breed
superior forms
of attention
that will outlast
efforts
to ignore it.
For hours
motorists queue
to fill tanks
like sheep hugging
electric fences.
Lightning makes
meat of cows
unexpectedly
mad and tree-bound.
Teenagers mutate

into blowflies,
travel like trains
without signals.

Year of the Rat

I'm not always able to miss people the way I feel I should,
the living and the dead: absences that leave me despairing
at their lack of presence, or my failure to preserve them in
memory, like astrologers' predictions before a year begins:

You will be travelling far and wide this year, so you can make more
of two or three very special plans. It's full speed ahead. Carve out
time to re-energize and reconnect. With persistence, a new normal
should begin to take shape. The rats will have a wonderful time.

Sometimes I call a number and then remember why there's
·no answer. Sometimes friends call me and I wonder if they
are also shocked when I pick up. 'Carve out time,' I think,
like a sculptor leaving timelessness corroding on a plinth.

Several people I never saw last year I will never see again,
the new normal. The rat population grew by thirty million.
Through scuttling and squeaks, a gallery view in my head,
I picture the statistics. I name them even as they fade.

The Rules

The tourists in the pasticceria are keen to showcase their flawless Italian. They ask their host how long she has worked here? What does she recommend? Has she ever been to Motherwell? Where was she born? They sound like they are reading a self-penned fifteenth century sonnet with a tin ear. She understands them, but her expression tells them something is wrong. They consult their phrasebook for the answers.

A couple of pigeons bully a child across a car park.

Here come the anti-vaxxers mourning
disruption to the normal protocols,
slumped behind the rose berry bush
they claim has no means to exist.

Are all the pages blank? Or is it just the way you read them?

You want to hear what I do? I wear a helmet only when I'm not riding my bike. I wear it on the sofa, when I'm sleeping in my drawer, when I gaze longingly into the dressing-table mirror. No one understands me.

His motto was 'always write more one book than you've read'.

He concentrates hard on the pizza box.
For him, it's an operator's manual.

Here come the experts bullying a child across a dictionary of formulae.

I have a theory about tuna and traffic
that roars by my house day and night.
I no longer notice the disturbance,
and the silent tuna many miles away
ignore the hooks reeling them in.

Monocle

C'mon, uncle! Your monocle
dropped from a raised eyebrow –
whether raised at the revealing
peignoir of Wallace Stevens
or the strained bonhomie
of wee Stevie Wallace,
the geometrical tat in Tati's
satire or the state of the Tate's
designer slate-grey tote –
dropped into dust with all
virtuosic nineteenth century
style – cravats, neckties, frock
coats, corsets, hessian boots –
and all fashion since until
only the present remained:
varifocals on prescription
from Boots, a single glass
slipper from Shoe Zone
that fits neither foot
but prints in rose-tint
if angled strategically
towards the Daily Slow
Motion replay of days
gone by – political history
dressed with accessories,
filling its own bunk with
highlights and footnotes:
itself lullabying itself
with one decisive voice.

The Forms

'we're practising forms of laughter/ life's other defiances'
NURDURAN DUMAN, translated by ARON AJI

The heehaw guffaw is an explosion, enough
to stop tourist traffic – click, flash – or more
likely, be politely ignored like a house alarm

braying through years of state-sponsored
burglary. Agitators in peacetime mobilize
sound-cancelling earphones in libraries

if the waggish electrodonkey disturbs their
contemplation. They are reading the latest
research into how influencers divide scorn

between snigger and grimace. Did you hear
the ruined millionaire licks gravy stains off
his linoleum? There are always audiences

gearing up to laugh with the crushed hearts
of darkened amusement parks. I'm the sort
to crush them further with a perfectly timed

jibe, but only in my mind. Did you know
Castro stubbed his iconic cigars on the outstretched
arms of the proletariat? But don't sneer,

it's all symptomatic of the revolutionary
endeavour to be sincere: property is theft,
robbery is self-care; education is exercise

in spin, the struggle session its discipline;
rhyme is for jingles, rhythm for textbook
angles on Stalin's diminutive schtick,

bound in human skin. There are forms to fill,
records to shred, a vast invisible history of
silent mirth requiring payment in lip service.

Did you read Jacob Rees-Mogg's dad's book
on how to giggle through eras of po-faced
disaster? It works! But I'm the sort to break

painfully into a grin for wedding photographs
only. I crave and fear sufficient insouciance
to laugh at the jokes running the country.

A Bad Morning for Radio 4

'[*The Archers*] finally ended after what felt like a year. Then it was _ _ _
_ _ _ _ on *Desert Island Discs*. She chose really boring songs. Now it's a
programme about dots in paintings. A bad morning for Radio 4.' – L.P.

The news is all disaster, the interviews accusation
and evasion. Later, some bloke talks about artistic
black holes and exquisitely cooked poems he claims
fail to work on so many levels: the level of lifesaving,
for example, or the half of writing that is marketing.
An author appears to be writing half his latest book
this morning without having to dream up a single
original word. He could regurgitate himself for hours.
Monologue is the level of pandemic communication –
The Archers talk to themselves about themselves:
they too have products for personalities, maybe
a sign of what a reset future holds: the broken past
continuous, spun to a level much worse than before.
A brand new Sting track backing adverts for Hovis
rouses the desert island's plastic palm branches
to clatter madly in nostalgia for the NHS whenever
storms sink rescue boats off the knife-edged coast.
Sting, Limp Bizkit, and a two-minute Mozart nugget
everyone knows from very level-headed instant
coffee campaigns, give way to dots on paintings:
a dramatic improvement in mood and interest-
level but not enough to challenge the morning's
dumpster-for-hire status and, the point is, it had
done its level best to convince us – eager listeners
of Radio 4 – that it was worth waking up to, worth
living another day as commodities and consumers

simultaneously, somehow worth trying to forge
a path as neither; and it, too, failed on every level
the way poems fail, paintings fail and all art fails
when we demand success, as if the world cannot
change until we have been given what we want.

Triptych

there was
nothing
the first joke
remained uncracked
awaiting delivery
and therefore optimistic
hilarity would ensue
to record our struggles
the tomfoolery which
like smoke
burnt-out buildings
spools from suffering
to perform it
with a splash of wit
and inevitably
God became jealous
of laughter
in secluded places
promoted distraction
in plain sight
to quench its power
made light of
sounding the alarm

in the beginning
God created
the heavens and the earth
the earth was formless
and empty
darkness was over
the surface of the deep
and the Spirit of God
was brooding over
the waters
and God said
let there be light
and there was light
God saw that
the light was good
and separated the light
from the darkness
God called the light 'day'
and the darkness
he called 'night'
and there was evening
and there was morning
the first day

a tall tale about
the original laugh track
and a border
like a blown eggshell
the slogan assured us
was no more than a facade
nothingness existed
to broadcast
us
our bodies were
comedy's highest achievement
and also cloud cover
giving shape to utterance
we lived for laughter
for nothing else
that stirred the flames
we cultivated
spun the earth and
made a god of it
needy for applause
the laugh track
like an aftershock
kept echoing within us

Faceback

for queasy hilarity
memory exhumes
the latest rising star's
old, monotonous story:
a cultivated persona
  will expose
the mess best forgotten –
            performatively
on-screen
            uninvited –
from this date
  decades ago

            but it seems

  decades on
from this date,
            uninvited
on-screen
  performatively,
a mess best forgotten
  will expose
the cultivated persona;
            old, monotonous story
            the latest rising star's
            memory exhumes
            for queasy hilarity

The Hour, the Hours

The hour the hours
await, passing by

＊

Not a *Te Deum*
but   virtuoso
    tedium   from
the sluggish organist

＊

The train is due.
Some optimists
  still   hang fire
    for the Messiah

＊

A little red demon with horns
paints your caricature
nailed to a tree.
No one cares. My work
is done, thinks the demon.

＊

Some think
horizons are illusory
   and beyond
       lies a great event
     the one
they've waited for
          all their lives

*

The dust has settled
but someone is always
ready to kick it up
     a plagiarist resurrection

*

I hear barking from the distance
     it's the past or future
happening now

*

between disappearances
different trains
flickering stars

*

Fans jostle before the game,
drink and sing,
   occupy the pavements
   like enemy armies.
        You once maintained
it was all about the journey

      *

The party demon offers you
an eternal loop, your life
   on repeat, the luxury
of no choices to make.
The choice is not yours

      *

A woman watches her soap
without earphones, puts
everyone in a rage
    airing
their private thoughts

      *

Not quite a *Te Deum*
     but an empty train
enters the radio station
        doors shut tight against
     the DJ's insistent blab
as usual

                    *

I used to think beans on toast
was the greatest meal
but when the sweet-toothed demon
promised a better tomorrow
I swallowed his tasteless pill

                    *

Five well-heeled hopefuls
hear the clock ticking,
        draw their rollerballs:
a poetry workshop on the how
and why
   and who
        and when
of today's popular culture

                    *

Two drunks scream at each other
on Great Junction Street –
    political discourse
uniting the government
                    in applause

                    *

Two dogs
    woof! *woof*! *woof*!
my thoughts
    the literal version
                    for translation

                    *

The dust has settled
    a great event
advertising itself

                    *

Take my hand. I've got the time
if you've got the money. Let's spend
both together and see who ends up
with spare change.

                    *

The demon thinks in yellow neon,
interrupts your sleep, offers
a chance to repeat your life
with three changes: you consider
height, weight, looks, offspring,
genitalia, personality, consciousness
and, implicitly, the price to be paid
for living the dream

*

I offer a *Te Deum*, prayers, puffs of smoke
but God is two seats ahead
watching a soap without earphones

*

The trains due
multiply in the parallel
shadows of themselves
arriving early, or late:
all our lives contained
within other lives

*

Within the dog
a clock barks

*

I tried to save time
by multitasking

spreading benevolence
like the grace of God

but tasks remain
ticking clocks assert

a right to silence
when arrested

*

The demon
as government
consultant
succeeds
planetary
extinction with
the DJ's
passion
for bisque

*

I miss those days
I could leave
   doors unlocked
   my pet dodo
off the leash

*

The hours the hour
fades into
   make me feel
less
   like a split   second

Very Civil Servant

Just as well I'm never on stage. I hate applause
that rewards obvious effort. It's exhausting,
their expectation of stimulus, my vainglorious
need to satisfy it. I've always fancied myself
as something of a comedian and can imagine
tone, catchphrase, signature walk-on salute –
without content: I can't remember jokes, and
just as well. My act is a sentence without words
or perhaps a life sentence for a murder victim.
I admit I am not a funny man, but I love being
thought of as funny: laughter not at or with
but like the homage of a temple sacrifice –
precious meat burning to feed my ridiculous
appetite. Let me recount a meaningless event
from yesterday that today becomes 'material'.
Or let's not. Just as well my demands are not
their demands. When they heckle, it always
feels like a half-arsed curtsey to traditional
bad behaviour, as if they've already accepted
the lack of reciprocity afterwards; my zinger
won't come till I'm stumbling home, drunk,
with all the panache and brio of clambering
from a pantomime horse's back-end. Just as
well no one will recall my humourless asides
delivered like blank slates to consumers out
of earshot on the High Street randan. I affect
the world only with white noise, tennis ball
countenance, mall muzak, background grift,
any loose hinge in a gate. Still, small silence.
My quips zip overhead like abandoned cabins,

business class. Just as well, they think, until
I let slip my plans, how they've already been
carried out without a moment's awareness.

The Circus Wars

Naturally, the clown mines his sorrows
like everyone else. He's fallen out with
the aging ringmaster whose subtlety
on morality confuses him. What *is* his
position on the cancelled contortionist?
How many twists and turns are allowed
before a body becomes less than a body?
How many fiery hoops will a ringmaster
squeeze through to defend the offence
the clown considers indefensible? Not
so much the opinions, but the affront
to express them with two feet stuck
firmly in each cheek. The crowd thought
the clown was smiling until gloopy tears
smudged his deep dinner-plate eye paint,
proving himself intrinsic to the troupe-
think constantly on edge: the acrobats'
pyramid collapses from the top down;
the bearded lady has alopecia; the clown,
when he trips over the elephant's trunk,
terrifies the little children by lying in
recovery position, stiff as a chalk outline;
his sidekicks start digging what looks
like a grave but heralds only a latterly
boundless program of trench warfare.
The ringmaster refuses to synthesize
the contortions. He makes the trapeze
artists nervy by stripping highly strung
concept junkies of their safety nets;
offends the lion-tamer and needlessly

provokes the starving, mangy lions,
who roar in rage at the very mention
of food sculpture workshops with
vegetarian, plant and balloon options.

The Biz

Ten years ago, it was bees.
Five, water.
And now, themselves.

They identify, without irony,
as 'creatives', as living
funding applications.

Petunias parade from a window pot.
The poets cut them, a final edit.

They get confused if you mention joy.

They write when the risk-takers
have synchronised agreement on outcomes.

They talk often about 'the industry'.
Sometimes, they explain the industry
to the industry.

Their work is mostly
network.

Between brief silences, they spread
generously
their bread and butter souls.

They look forward to the end of meaningful existence.
They have lived a perfect metaphor.

My Farm

Because a true poet possesses transferable skills
and ten thousand hours of staring at blank screens
to note the detail others pass over, I have decided,
this time next year, to become a farmer.
                                        I will gorge
on dawn breakfasts with my ravenous Turkish friend
Gustav, who also has no direct experience of farms,
but his wife is expert in enclosing feta in fat wallets
of pastry. Yes, excess is required before the sun
spits over our fields.
                        I cannot drive, but I am certain,
just as Michael Caine developed consumer confidence
in Mini Coopers when they tore up the luxury mall
of via Roma in *The Italian Job*, you'll find the humble
tractor trending on the bulletin boards when I tow
mounds of stinking hay to village fête lawns in late
summer.
            I will cultivate potatoes, the Jim Davidson
of vegetables – tasteless, valueless, unaccountably
ubiquitous in post-Brexit bistros – and feed them
to my goats as they stroll the hills like presidents
without countries to rule over. The dogs will feed
on sheep, the cows on milk, the pigs on bat shit,
the bats on any poor sprite that crawls or flies
through my sulphurous barns.
                                    I will maintain
an obsession with livestock: the skeletal hyenas,
pink mice lashed into bubblegum or blancmange,
cigar-puffing Siamese, cider-swilling rats, gibbons
on social media twenty hours a day arguing that

cannabis is dangerously addictive. I will farm them
into data, algorithmic spaghetti.

        I will conduct
rooster choirs while Gustav scans his news menu
for signs of weakness in the chickenfeed economy:
so much to exploit, so little time to be bothered,
but smallholders and urban dandies form the grit
from which my oxgang expands.

        I long to daub
their chestnut crops with insecticide and novichok,
slide into occupied land, bundle manure and corn
into burnt offerings for pop idols. I will harness
unsung technology to wither the cities to fern
and bracken: Commodore 64, the dial-up modem,
Windows 95. Only the most implausible notions
have sufficient repercussions for the real world.

Recipes

I got so sick of the left eating itself, while a right-wing appetite for power
fed its bodily functions and expense accounts on a strict diet of more

than you can afford, that I suggested a cheap option, broad bean risotto,
because it took a lot of stirring, and you replied with gusto 'ditto, ditto'

as if commitment to culinary slumming might randomly marinate a recipe
for social upheaval. I feared we were in free fall, like pigs over a precipice,

soon to reconstitute on the rocks below as pork scratchings, imagining
nothing had changed except perspective. It appeared that I was legion,

not singular; manufactured, not opinionated; every thought I shared
had first been aired by a bored Russian cybermarketeer and every word

in the lesser songs of Celine Dion. I was a typical low-energy iconoclast
insisting on a high supply of soft-target icons. My influence collapsed

after my economy three-ingredient bacon roll was tainted by complete
absence of bacon, and no excuse I offered – health, savings, corporate

bull – was enough to satisfy the Hungry from Manchesters of this world
with ravenous demands for ruin. The right-wing, emboldened, stilled

their hi-salt blootered hearts. For the first time in decades, they slept,
pigs in blankets, for four straight hours, while envy snacked on the left.

New Puritan

The League of New Puritans
are waiting for the few
who gladly sign any dotted line.
We'll open doors for you.

Our ensign is a turtle dove
trussed up on a spit;
when suffering's running low on love
we get off on it.

Meetings begin with a list of sins,
the blocks we have achieved
(wishful thinking for most of us,
the holy self-deceived).

We godly gentlefolk explain,
expose, exfoliate;
clip juicy beards to style our pain
after we masturbate.

We deny ourselves, tame vanity,
are good, almost *too* good.
A full-page spread's just a fantasy;
we'll settle for partially nude.

We strip, get whipped and hang in hope
of extra flagellation;
a self-loathing swagger lets rip
our impotent aggression.

Everyone's welcome in our lodges
for unpolluted minds.
Everyone's welcome, except the radges
who tell us to be kind.

Meetings conclude in all-out war
though we're useless in a fight;
we waste and wound by snub and sneer
till everyone knows we're right.

And we're *always* right, *never* wrong
on all sides of all questions;
we'll deal with the deviant contretemps
after the insurrection.

We're theoretical feminists
who never rinse the dishes
or know the washing machine exists,
but we lecture on such mysteries.

We're theoretical socialists
with Oxbridge PhDs.
Working class Brexit enthusiasts
clearly have brain disease:

those doppelgänger-minded dipshits
emerged like all things Aryan
to goose up a special kinship
with the vox totalitarian.

We'll line them up against the wall,
reintroduce the birch.
We'll beat them black and blue until
they know their privilege

and know the age of revolution
is here, and we're in charge.
We're the headfuck and the solution,
the feeble-minded purge.

We're outraged by the price of piss,
electricity and sex,
and especially at the shrinking mass
of Cadbury's Creme Eggs.

As for the mainstream media,
especially the BBC,
the *Guardian* and *Wikipedia* –
we'll ban them permanently.

We're outraged by world views
that interrogate our own;
it's wrong if folk aren't forced to know
the burn of being wrong.

We're outraged charity doesn't begin
at home, like Jesus said,
and if he didn't, he should have done –
he wouldn't have ended up dead.

From the I I I to the Me Me Me
we divine our range of interests,
cherry-picking causes carefully
to diversify our influence.

We're Machiavellian even where
we claim no compromise;
our motto is 'We'll aye be whaur
extremes rule and divide.'

The League of New Puritans
plan a recruitment drive
for sadomasochist miscreants –
you may as well apply,

as this poem is a paroxysm
of hate made manifest
in the pseudo-moral dogmatism
we affect to be against.

A space to rest in piety
and flay ourselves as well;
a pandemonium publicly
to mask a private hell.

The Mix

I kept having this awful feeling that people thought
I was in the mix and, despite my best intentions,
maybe I was.

    It was hard to tell, due to my Gen X
designer minimalism and straitened circumstances
but the mix was like a giant vacuum that sucked
all life out of everyone and anything.

          Was I alive?
To some people, it appeared not, which pleased me
immensely; I didn't have to feature in their endless
conturbations on community, hierarchy and pretense
of acting without ambition or envy; on out and in;
on invisible lines they liked to draw and draw upon
whenever the virtues of a hard border appeared
utilitarian or unacknowledged.

       I was more of a tree
than a human being, but not the kind they thought
to cross hearts and carve initials on, not in any way
fit to bear the written word they flashed like an axe
or a riot shield.

      I will admit, although it's hard, I like
to belong. I ask myself if I should play a part in a raft,
a forest, a fireplace. Or, mixing my metamorphoses,
to occupy a branch as crow or vulture, even stuffed
like a dodo. Or to pass my final days in Chicken Club
as a philosophical fowl interrogating my nature
amid the deep-fat fryers; plotting elaborate coups
d'état and then seeking asylum in Chicken Cottage
across the road: avian chesterfields and davenports,
pearly eggcups, Skövby table extensions available

for hourly rent and renegade hen parties, beyond all
dreams of disposable income, beyond a joke.
                                           So, why
did the chicken cross the perimeter and leave the rest
squawking in solidarity?
                         Solidarity meaning solidarity
exclusively together: the statue they built from my
feathers was like a rag doll mixed with voodoo pins;
they clucked of blowing up my photograph but no one
clarified whether this involved a planned expansion
or destruction; they were transfixed by their own
reflections and pecked them in petroleum rainbows,
stained-glass puddles; they demanded the removal
of pens from community prisons, munched hardbacks
for breakfast and laid burnt, origami omelettes for
disappointing suppers on straw.
                                 In the mix, the only
art with cultural cachet is opinion; the only art with
cultural cash is hype; the only art with cultural cache
is influence.
              The mix was no zoo. It contained just
one species, previously undiscovered: human, with
the heart and voice of a Build-a-Bear – its wardrobe,
style, name, and constitutional identity – chosen with
care among a slew of limited options, which really
was no choice at all.
                       I had this awful feeling –
while I made lists of who was in the mix and aimed
my slingshot of blank verse at their backsides,
their lists were just mixtapes with me on them.

Lasting Chance

There was no saloon,
extra time snapshot,
or flotsam accessible
to outstretched arms
while Storm Abaddon
detonated the waves
like fireworks
and Wham! supplied
their Christmas hit
as soundtrack for
generations disposed
to theatrical expiry;
no bearded evangelist,
fresh from a last
supper in Burger King,
barking in tongues
that God's mysterious
lack of apocalyptic
closure was simply
an example to us all;
no priest to hear
the confession,
his eyes like spinning
platters of cocaine,
before hell's three
headed canine gate-
keeper scrambled
the six-figure divinely
expired entry code;

no last chance but
a chance that lasts
long enough to
make all deadline
calculators redundant
as logarithms
or movie sequels,
and outlives futile
popular culture
references entering
my eschatological
speculative verse
like a Tindersticks
ballad surreptitiously
scoring a shoot-out
for hard-boiled TV
gangster surrealism.
This opportunity
won't last forever
like those pearls –
the Kingdom of God,
and *Blue Peter* –
but it runs past
its sell-by date,
a long-distance
runner lapping itself,
spaghetti loops
unravelling constant
tributes to mortality,

multiple choice,
unfinished business,
bins, bottles, other
last chances.

Notes

Goldfish

this is a sonnenzio, https://poetscollective.org/everysonnet/sonnenzio/ and begins with the tenth line from George Mackay Brown's poem 'Sonnet: Hamnavoe Market'.

'Hopkins and Hill' – the poets Gerard Manley Hopkins and Geoffrey Hill, who lived in different centuries, but both had their famous Goldengrove moments.

Portobello Beach

the line 'Go sad or sweet or riotous with beer' is from George Mackay Brown's 'The Old Women'. The form is stolen from his poem 'The Laird'.

Arthur's Seat

'thousand candles of gorse' is from George Mackay Brown's poem, 'The Storm'.

Year of the Rat

The second stanza comprises of quotations from astrology websites predicting how things would go in the year ahead, 2020

Triptych

The middle column is *Genesis* 1:1–5. The poem should read both horizontally and vertically.

Acknowledgements

Thanks are due to the editors of the following magazines, where poems or versions of them were first published:

The Dark Horse, 14 *Magazine*, *The Friday Poem*, *Gutter*, *London Magazine*, *Northwords Now*, *One Hand Clapping*, *Raceme*, *Shearsman*.

'Portobello Beach' appeared in *Beyond the Swelkie*, edited by Jim Mackintosh and Paul S. Philippou, an anthology of poems and prose inspired by George Mackay Brown.

'New Puritan' was first published in the online project, *Gude and Godlie Ballatis*, edited by W.N. Herbert and Andy Jackson.

This book has been typeset by
SALT PUBLISHING LIMITED
using Sabon, a font designed by Jan Tschichold
for the D. Stempel AG, Linotype and Monotype Foundries.
It is manufactured using Holmen Book Cream 70gsm,
a Forest Stewardship Council™ certified paper from the
Hallsta Paper Mill in Sweden. It was printed and bound
by Clays Limited in Bungay, Suffolk, Great Britain.

CROMER
GREAT BRITAIN
MMXXIII